Lillenas Drama

Making a Name for Myself

Monologues with a Biblical Point of View

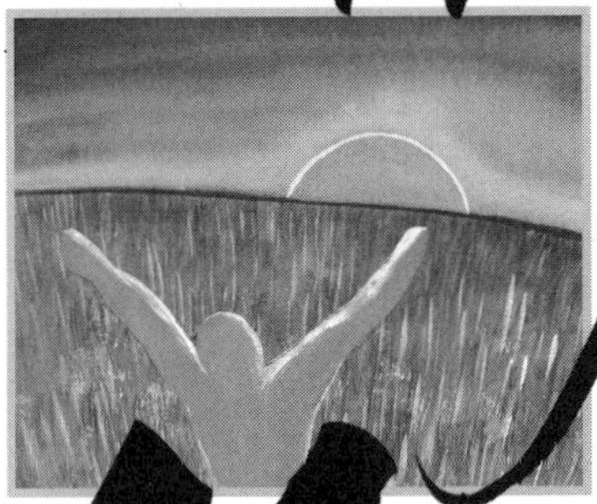

by Jill M. Richardson

KANSAS CITY, MO 64141

❖ **NOTE: New photocopy policy effective January 1, 1999.** ❖

The purchase of this book entitles the purchaser the right to make photocopies of this material for use in a church or a nonprofit organization. Sharing of the material in this book with other churches or organizations not owned or controlled by the original purchaser is prohibited. The contents of this book may not be reproduced in any other form without written permission from the publisher. Please include the copyright statement on each copy made.

Making a Name for Myself

Copyright © 1998 by Jill M. Richardson. All rights reserved. All print rights administered by Lillenas Publishing Co.

Unless marked, all Scripture quotations are from the *Holy Bible, New International Version*® (NIV®). Copyright © 1973, 1978, 1984 by International Bible Society. Used by permission of Zondervan Publishing House. All rights reserved.

King James Version (KJV)

Printed in the United States.

PLEASE READ CAREFULLY this is copyright material. It is illegal to copy this material by any means except under the conditions listed below. Amateur performance rights are granted when one copy of this book is purchased. You may duplicate individual sketch scripts from this book for $2.00 per copy with a maximum payment of $12.00 per individual sketch.

Please mail your request, payment, and information to:
    Lillenas Publishing Company
    Drama Permission Desk
    P.O. Box 419527
    Kansas City, MO 64141
    phone: 816-931-1900 • fax: 816-753-4071
    E-mail: drama@lillenas.com
    Information: Title, source, and author(s) of script(s)

Cover art by Ted Ferguson

CONTENTS

Introduction 5

Through Mary's Eyes 7

Ministers Anonymous 9

A Second Death 11

The Weight of Hate 13

Making a Name for Myself 16

If I Had It to Do Over Again...18

Seeing Is Believing 20

Lonely at the Top 23

The Morning After 25

One-Man Woman..27

Love, Honor, . . . and Obey?...29

Who Was That Man? 31

Catch Me Later 33

The Things Time Changes 35

Such a Deal 37

When I Grow Up 39

Who Cares About Aunt Leah? 41

A Simple Question 43

The Once—and Future?—King..45

In His Hands 47

INTRODUCTION

Drama—it's the way to go in the church! It speaks to a new audience, a fresh generation. You have to join the crowd!

But what about your church? You know—the one with 65 people, all working as hard as they can just to maintain what you've got going? The church where drama talent, or at least volunteerism, drags. Where a production of eight characters, or even four, is beyond the realm of imagination? The church where time to rehearse, organize, and orchestrate more than one or two people just needs to be used elsewhere?

These scripts are written for you, because I know where you are. One person is all you need. One person who wants to transmit, in a powerful way, that the questions of today, with all their contemporary problems and trappings, still find their answers in the Bible. Of course, if your church has 100 people, or 300, or 500, these are for you too. Busyness is not confined to the few.

These monologues are biblical in that they all spring from people in the Bible. Some, however, are created characters—people who must have been there but who remain anonymous in the record. The accuracy-obsessed will cringe at the abundance of anachronisms in these sketches. No, the rich young man probably did not drive a Jeep Cherokee, and Laban never heard of Chicago. But isn't it a great beauty of Christianity that an eternal God can blend old and new together in a timeless bond?

I suggest contemporary dress for the characters. The point of each sketch is to say that these people who lived long ago have something important to tell us now. Therefore, playing them in biblical costume defeats this purpose. It will convey the "long ago" aspect all too clearly, especially to the person not well acquainted with the Bible, leaving behind the "now." Think of what each person would wear if she or he lived today. Mary's best friend—the lower middle class teen. Zaccheus—the successful businessman. Gomer—the call girl.

Often the character speaks to someone else on the scene. There should never be another person actually present. The person must help the audience imagine the other party and sometimes help them be the other party.

Similarly, props should be kept to a minimum. The audience should be led to imagine they are there by the movement of the character. They need not be actually seen and probably shouldn't be. So, Dorcas only holds up imaginary clothing. Some exceptions, of course, can be made. The rich young man is more effective when one can see the size of his piles and hear their shuffle and clink. Moses needs a basket. But most other characters needn't use anything but their voice and movement to create the scene.

By the way, I dislike terms like "audience" and "stage" for a church setting.

(God is our audience, and the congregation should never be spectators at a performance!) But they have been necessary in the suggestions for use of these sketches. If you hate them, too, just bear with them and substitute what you will.

Enjoy, and God bless your worship of Him, for He alone is worthy.

THROUGH MARY'S EYES

Theme: What does it mean to have "God with us"? Are we ready for the baby of Christmas to truly come into our lives?

Passage: Luke 1:26-35

Character: Mary's best friend

Related Scripture: Psalm 34:1-10; John 1:1-14; Hebrews 1:1-3

Suggestions for Use: Mary's best friend would be an older teen or young woman. She should wear a plain dress (or pants and shirt) with no frills, and flat, simple shoes. She doesn't want excitement, and her clothes should show that.

I wanted to believe her. After all, she's my best friend. But this was a lot wilder than any of the stories we used to make up as girls playing in the fields. We made up some good ones back then, Mary and I did. All about palaces and princes and following the camel trains to who knows where. But she wasn't playing this time. She told me she was going to have a baby. But not any ordinary baby. *God's* Baby. God's Son.

I can't forget her face when she told me. At first she was shy, kind of uncertain. But then, she just turned so . . . so radiant. Her eyes shone, and she had this smile. Just this hint of a smile. It kind of said, "Please, share my wonderful secret." I couldn't believe it. No shame. No repentance. She sat there telling me—me, her best friend who's shared everything for years—telling me that she's still a virgin and yet pregnant by the Spirit of God.

I mean, we all hope for the Messiah. My papa prays for Him to come three times a day! But surely if God wanted to send Him He'd choose something a little more . . . believable. Something a little less . . . disreputable. The Messiah will be strong, powerful, a mighty warrior for His people. We girls may not go to school, but we know *that*. And this Child of Mary's . . . no father, a mother poorer than poor, from a little one-camel town in backwoods Judea. And the things people will *say* about him! "Mary," I said. "It's me, Abby. Your best friend. How can you expect me to believe a story like this? How stupid do you think I am? How could you even tell me such a whopper? I would never lie to you."

Then I looked in her eyes again. They were shining and joyful still. But I could see something else too. Mary was afraid. My best friend—and she looked so scared in spite of all her excited talk. She started to say something, but then she just turned and left. I couldn't go after her. I couldn't believe her.

But yet . . . These questions keep nagging me. What about Joseph? Why didn't he divorce her? He's sticking by her story, every bit of it, holding his head high. I mean, couldn't he just have married her quietly? And if it's really not his baby—why I can just imagine what my fiancé Jacob would do! But Joseph hardly says a word, just looks kind of peculiar and says quietly, "Mary doesn't lie." Why?

Then there are Elizabeth and Zechariah. You don't get much closer to God than those two. And *they* believe her. There's also this strange feeling I get whenever I look in her eyes. This burning in my heart. I half-wish, half-fear she's telling the truth. Could it be true? *Could* God have chosen here, and now, and her? Could He be sending the One we've all been waiting for?

Oh Mary, maybe you're afraid, but I am too! The Messiah was a nice dream when it was just that—a dream. But when it's flesh and blood, God right here and now, *nothing* will ever be the same. Your world may have been turned upside down, Mary. But if what you say is true, ours will be too. My life may not be as exciting as my dreams when we were kids, but it works for me. I'm engaged. I'll be settled. I'll live a normal life. What would it mean to have God invade my life? Not just in prayers and fasts and chants and feasts, but in bones and skin, and right there?

But I can't forget her eyes. That joy in them. The joy that even my taunts couldn't shake. So steady—even when her best friend refused to believe her. Maybe that's what she was about to say when she left. She has something I don't have. She knows something I don't know. Or maybe, Someone?

MINISTERS ANONYMOUS

Theme: Serving in humility

Passage: Ephesians 6:21-22

Character: Tychicus (ti-ki-kus)

Related Scripture: Philippians 2:1-16; 3:3-11; Luke 14:7-11; John 3:25-31; Ecclesiastes 2:22, 24-25; 3:9-13, 22

Suggestions for Use: Props could include a stamped letter and a shoulder sack for letters and traveling necessities. Tychicus walked a lot. He needs clothes that are comfortable, tough, and nondescript.

Hi. I'll bet you don't know me. I'd tell you my name, but well, you probably wouldn't recognize it. That's OK. I'm used to it. Everyone knows the guy I work with a little better than me. His name? It's Paul. 'Nuf said, huh? Everywhere we go, it's "Oh Paul, welcome to our church, welcome to our home; we're so honored to have you . . ." Then they turn to me, and I can see their faces go blank. "And you're . . . what was your name again?" they ask. I just smile and remind them. "It's Tychicus," I say. "Just call me 'Brother Ty.'"

I couldn't always smile, you know. I guess you might say I used to be a bit competitive. I remember the time in school Tony memorized more of the *Iliad* than I had. I got so mad, I cut his toga sash on the way home, right in the middle of Market Square. Never saw a boy run so fast in my life. Too bad it wasn't racing season. Then there was Alexander, who swore he'd marry the beautiful Julia before I could. Don't like to tell you what I did then. Wasn't very Christian, you know.

But somehow, these days, it doesn't bother me a bit to be referred to as "that fellow who delivers Paul's mail." It's kind of funny, isn't it? I'm a nobody now and perfectly happy. In those days when I was trying so hard to be a somebody, I was never happy at all. There was always someone better. Someone who knew more, someone who married a prettier girl, someone who was stronger or faster or richer. Every time I got what I thought I wanted, there was something more to get.

Then Paul burst into my life. He understood. He *had* had it all. I remember. "Garbage!" he told me. "Just garbage, Tychicus. Toss it all away! Don't you know you'll never be anything until you admit you're nothing? Why are you trying to impress people? Don't you know the God of the universe is waiting for your life? Not some mere human! The Lord and Creator of all wants *you*, as you are. You don't have to be anything. In fact, Tychicus, you've got to stop trying."

I don't think I can tell you how that made me feel. God—almighty God himself—just loved me, failures and all. I had spent my whole life thinking it was my name that mattered most, my achievements that made life worthwhile. Now suddenly I realized there's only one Name that matters. And only a life given to Him is ever worthwhile.

It was the toughest thing I've ever done, admitting I couldn't make it on my own. But it felt so great to stop trying. To step right into His loving embrace. And all those things I wanted to be? I'm a child of the King of the universe. One of the King's greatest men, Paul, calls me "brother." I've been promised an inheritance beyond all imaginable wealth. All I had to do was give up myself. A pretty good trade since, to be honest, what I was wasn't so great.

Now I'm a letter carrier. But I don't just deliver Paul's letters. I deliver God's words. And no one knows my name. I don't expect that will ever change. Just call me "Brother Ty." But you don't have to remember that. I don't mind.

A SECOND DEATH

Theme: Faith in painful circumstances

Passage: John 19:16-30

Character: Lazarus

Related Scripture: Psalms 13; 22:1-5; Lamentations 3:21-26; Luke 23:26, 32-49

Suggestions for Use: A Good Friday (pre-Easter) monologue. Lazarus stands at the Cross, in utter disbelief. He will not move much at all; his shock keeps him still.

Someone tell me it's a dream! He's not dying! He can't die! How can the Man who gave me life die—like He's any other human being? Don't you people know who that is up there on that cross? Dear God—do I know?

I thought I did. It was so clear on that day I came walking out of the tomb. How can I describe what it felt like to enter that dark valley of death one minute, the fearful walls closing in on me, and to be alive again the next—more alive than ever before?

When I heard that voice—"Lazarus, come forth!"—I knew who it was. I knew, stronger and surer than I ever had in life, who it was. Jesus. Not just my friend Jesus but my Lord Jesus. The voice compelled me, and I never had any choice but to obey. His was the first face I saw when they unwrapped the cloths from my eyes. And I knew. The people who saw gasped. Then they sang and danced. And believed. And so did I. That wasn't so long ago! Don't they remember? Hey—He raised me from the dead! Me—Lazarus! You saw it! Hey, people! You were there! What are you doing? How could this happen?

I remember the words He spoke to my sister Martha that day. "I am the Resurrection and the Life. Whoever believes in Me will live even if he dies, and everyone who lives and believes in Me will never die." He spoke of *being* life. Of never dying. But how does it all fit together with this? Jesus, how can You be the Resurrection and the Life, up there on that cross, gasping for air, blood-smeared and beaten? What did You mean? Why did You save me and not yourself? Why are You letting them do this?

Martha said something else to Him that day. "Lord, if You had been here, my brother would not have died. Even now I know that whatever You ask of

God, God will give You." She really didn't understand why He hadn't come to save me. Her grief overwhelmed most of her thoughts. She still had enough to feel a little angry, though, and a lot confused. A lot like I feel now. But she trusted Him anyway. She believed.

I knew who You were then. I know now. I just don't understand. God, help me to understand! I know who You are. But I don't know why this is happening to You.

I thought my own death was the darkest valley I would ever walk. Jesus, Yours is much darker. So terribly, horribly dark. But You are still the Resurrection and the Life, whatever that means. God, I wish I could open my eyes and find this all a dream. Just help me to know it isn't a mistake.

THE WEIGHT OF HATE

Theme: Self-revelation and forgiveness

Passage: Luke 19:1-10

Character: Zacchaeus

Related Scripture: Psalm 51; Ezekiel 33:14-16; Proverbs 28:13-14; Lamentations 3:40-42

Suggestions for Use: Zacchaeus is probably middle-aged. Though he was small, size is not a major issue in casting. Perhaps someone over six feet would be less believable, but neither must you search for someone unusually small. He is traditional and wealthy, and should dress in "traditional" Sunday best, conservative manner.

Don't give me credit for anything special. Some folks have said I wanted to change my ways. Some say I must have really loved God in my heart. They figure I must have had a good motive for going to such lengths to see Jesus—climbing that tree and all. Otherwise, He'd have never noticed me, much less gone to my home. But that's the thing about Jesus—He never needed a reason to love somebody. That's something most people can't understand, that kind of love. I sure didn't understand it. He would never have found a reason to love me. I hadn't loved anyone else in a long, long time.

I was pretty young when I got sick—about six. I didn't understand why Mother cried when she looked at me or why Father stopped looking at me at all. I just figured I'd get better. But then it started getting harder and harder to walk. Or to do anything else. I couldn't run and play with the other boys. People laughed when I climbed the tree to see Jesus. But there was a time when no one thought I'd ever climb a tree again.

I got better, but my body was never the same. My arms and legs looked shriveled and thin, and they didn't work so well. I walked kind of hunched and limping, always smaller than the others. I tried to play, but I always hit the ball the wrong way, or tripped over someone's foot, or was the first one to get caught out. They laughed at me. My friends, at least I'd thought they were. They pointed and called me names and laughed so hard to see me limping along, losing every game by a mile. I quit trying finally. It just hurt too much.

Mother kept trying, working to help me walk better. And it did help. But

Father still never looked at me. I knew why. Even that young, I knew. I had disappointed him. His son, his first son. I would never be strong and tall and popular. I would never take my place at the city gates and make him proud. He was probably afraid I'd end up a beggar there instead. He was ashamed of me, and I felt ashamed too.

So I decided I'd get them. I'd show them all. I started to use the one thing that worked well—my mind. I learned. I became one of the best students in Hebrew school. Not *the* best—they'd never allow a lame boy to be the best. But I was good. And I stored up every hurt, every cruel word, every push from behind that sent me sprawling in the dirt, every condescending look. And I swore they'd pay for them all.

So tax collecting just came kind of natural when the Romans offered it to me. I had no loyalties to "my people." They'd made it clear they didn't want me to be one of them. At last I'd found a way to make them pay, literally. The Romans let me keep whatever I collected over their cut. So I collected a lot. The more someone had hurt me, the more money I demanded. They couldn't say no. I built the biggest house around, from their money. But I lived in it alone. No matter how rich I got, no one would let his daughter marry me. Zacchaeus, the lame traitor. I hated them for their taunts. But I hated myself, too, because I knew I had become just as bad as they said I was. I knew my heart was more black and shriveled than my bones had ever been. But why try to change? No one was going to care for me any more if I did.

When I heard Jesus was coming, I thought, big deal. No tax base there. He's poorer than a beggar's donkey. But I was intrigued. He had a reputation for being everything I wasn't. He gave when people took from Him. He forgave when people spat at Him. He loved when they made it clear they didn't want Him around. I had to see what made Him work. I didn't believe it could be true. No mere man could act that way. What was in it for Him?

It was awfully hard to climb that tree. My arms and legs ached with every stretch they weren't used to making. But I knew I could never see Him in all those people if I stayed on the ground. I didn't mind the people laughing at me. I was used to that.

The group of tired-looking men and women approached down the road, and I could hear the crowd getting excited below me. Excited? For this man? He hardly looked worth it. What was so wonderful about this dust-covered, untrimmed man?

Then I saw Him. Or to put it more accurately, He saw me. He looked up, and He looked at me. And I saw . . . I saw the look I'd always longed for. I saw the look I'd yearned for my own father to give me. People were always looking around me, or above me, or through me. But he looked at me, with eyes that had every right to condemn but loved instead. If I thought I'd seen the darkness of my own heart before, I saw it then in even more painful detail. All those years believing I had the right to hate, to get even, to weigh out my grudges against humanity on the scales of shekels. Now here was One who had the right to judge us all, and He forgave me instead. He didn't have to tell me to repent. It was done before I reached the ground.

Nor did He have to tell me what to do next. I knew what I had done. I knew what I owed. I couldn't consider paying what I owed Him, but I could make a start on everyone else. And suddenly, I wanted to. He was handing me the chance to take the burdens of those grudges carried around for years and hurl them as far away as superhuman strength could hurl. I wanted that chance. I wanted to live free and clean. I wanted to learn to love.

So don't believe I had some great motive of goodness for climbing to see Him. I didn't. Don't think I was an incredible saint for giving back so much more than I'd taken. I wasn't. It was freedom to be rid of gains that weren't mine, from hate I no longer owned. My body is still the way it's always been. But my heart is healed.

MAKING A NAME FOR MYSELF

Theme: The foolishness of the Cross; God's idea of success often conflicts with how we might plan.

Passage: Mark 8:27-37

Character: Judas

Related Scripture: 1 Corinthians 1:18-25; Proverbs 16:25; Matthew 11:25-27; Job 38—39

Peter was right. Jesus is going over the edge. What in the world was He talking about—prophesying His own death like He had some special way of knowing? Here we were, innocently walking down the road, having a stimulating discussion. Then He starts this death talk. And He sounded like He meant it would be soon. He thinks the religious leaders are going to kill Him? Well, it would help if He'd stop baiting them so much. Get their power on our side. He never takes the right advantages. I've always told Him He had to be smarter that way. But the worst part of it all was that He talked about His death like it was something He *wanted* to happen.

Peter had more guts than the rest of that bunch. He came out and said it. "Of course You're not going to die. What a stupid thought! What will happen to all we've done? All the good we've accomplished? What will happen to us?"

Then Jesus got really strange and started talking about Satan, like he was there or something. He turned on Peter. Peter—his right-hand man! How safe could the rest of us be after that? I think that's when I started to realize things were going sour. I never bargained for this death talk.

I followed Jesus because I could see He was a winner. He could be something. Sure, He was a bit rough around the edges. He liked to hang out with the wrong set of people. His language needed a little culture. That's to be expected of the riffraff of Galilee. But there was something there—I sensed it. My winner's instinct said, "Go for it."

And *this* was it? Some talk about violent death and the end of it all—for no purpose? I wanted to yell, "Hey! Get off Peter's case! He's right! Don't throw away all we've worked for!"

But I didn't, because suddenly I could see I'd backed the wrong horse. How galling to admit it. Me, the man who had always picked the winners. Will I get out of this with one shred of dignity left? Maybe . . . maybe I could still get something out of all of it. Three years worth of investment! Can't I still possibly break even? There's got to be a way for an industrious guy like me.

I've got a future ahead of me. I'm going places. Die? You could be king, Jesus. You could have everything. You could get whatever You asked for from these people. What good will You do any of us dead? What kind of king can You be then? Where is this kingdom You're always talking about—in the grave?

He's not a winner at all. He's a loser. A failure. Twenty years from now no one will remember His name. But me—I'm not letting this slow me down. I've got places to go. They'll remember the name of Judas.

IF I HAD IT TO DO OVER AGAIN

Theme: Making daily living count. Often our tendency is to concentrate on emotional thrills and miss the day-to-day discipleship of living for Jesus. If we died as this woman did, and were also raised, would our lives have been such that we wouldn't change a thing when we started over?

Passage: Acts 9:36-42

Character: Dorcas/Tabitha

Related Scripture: Ephesians 5:15-17; Matthew 24:45-47

Suggestions for Use: Dorcas is an older woman. (Fifty-something was old then, though not now!) After her initial paragraph (likely said at a door or window), she can be seated. Perhaps she will look through her piles of clothes or cloth as she talks.

What a lovely day this would be to get out. No more rain, but it's not yet too hot for an old lady like me. The clothes have been piling up a bit. The others are real good about delivering them for me. I can still make them quicker than anyone, but I do miss bringing them around.

I used to love taking some new thing to one of the ladies down in the poor section—just to see how happy it made her. Or a few outfits to the children. They were always so thankful for whatever they got. Perhaps I could just pop out the back door and no one would see me. Even do a little shopping around . . . maybe some cloth from Julia down the way. She has such lovely things. Always gives me a discount, too, since it's for a good cause. Why not?

But what would I do if the crowds come again? It's just too much for me, all their pushing up close—right in my face—to ask their questions. I'm not used to attention. I don't like crowds. I just want to live quietly the way I always have. But I can't seem to get away from them ever since . . .

No one paid this much attention to me when I was alive. Well, alive for the first time, I mean. But now . . . now, it seems . . . so strange, so funny. *I'm* the one who died. I'm the one Peter came and woke up to come back to the living. And yet . . . yet it seems they've all gone crazy, and I'm the only one who hasn't changed.

Every day, every time I walk outside it's: "Hey! Dorcas! What was it like? Tell us, tell us! What did you see? What did you do? Was it weird? Was it scary? Was it, was it, was it?" They never seem to get tired of wanting to know what it's like to die. Even when I tell them I don't remember, that it's all like a darkened dream to me now. They still ask, hoping they'll be the lucky ones to make me remember.

But I don't want to remember! I want to remember living, not dying! Some said I couldn't have had much of a life. No husband, no children, no money. But I did. Each time I sewed a stitch in a new dress, I thought about the smiles I'd see from the one who would wear it. Each time I took an extra hour to embroider something a little special, a small speck of beauty, on clothes I knew some woman would wear who had never seen much beauty. Each time my sisters in Jesus sat down with me to a feast filled with love, if not too grand otherwise, I knew it was a good life. I wasn't afraid to die when I got sick. I knew my Jesus would care for me. But I did love living.

Of course the miracle was incredible. Thank God—I'm alive again! I *am* grateful. It *is* something to talk about! But how can I talk about it and make them see, not gape? They only want the fanfare, the flashing lights, the laser show. But what about the fifty-some years I lived before all that? What about all the quiet parts of life that make up that show at the end?

I just want to go on doing the things I did before I died. Making clothes for the poor. Taking unnoticed walks to the shops. The things that made me happy. The things that made Him happy. But no one asks me about those things. They all want to know what it's like to die. Doesn't anyone want to know what it's like to live?

SEEING IS BELIEVING

Theme: Trusting God requires a real experience with Him. We do not inherit faith; we find it in meeting Him for ourselves.

Passage: Joshua 6:1-20

Character: An Israelite at Jericho

Related Scripture: John 20:24-29; 2 Corinthians 4:16-18; Hebrews 11; Psalm 20

Suggestions for Use: Here is an anonymous participant in the famous events of Joshua 6. What did the average Joe (or Levi) think of God's battle plan? He dresses in average clothing as well. A casual shirt and jeans or casual pants will work better than a Sunday suit and tie.

I was born out there in the desert wilderness. I figured I'd die there too. I never really understood what made my parents begin that mad, long walk. They used to talk a lot about what it had been like in Egypt. Working the whole day as slaves, sweating and bleeding for other people's comfort, watching brothers and sisters beaten and dying. Sometimes they wondered if it was worth getting up in the morning again. They made bricks for the Egyptians, so my parents said. It was kind of hard for me to imagine making bricks. There's not a lot of water in the desert for that kind of work. There's not a lot of anything, as a matter of fact. Just the same endless wilderness, for a long, long time.

I didn't used to think they'd made a very good trade. Life may have been tough in Egypt, but was this monotonous wandering any better? At least they had good food there. Enough water, and a place all their own. I asked them about it a lot—especially just before they died. "Why did you do it, Mom and Dad? Why did you follow that bearded dreamer Moses into *this?* Back there, you could have died old, in your own home. At least you'd have had some comfort, if not dignity. Why?" I must have asked them 12 times a day. I'd never lived in Egypt. Could it really have been that bad?

They didn't answer. They just gazed up at the huge cloud ahead of us and got this look in their eyes. They said, "God handled the sea, my son. He can handle the desert too." But I didn't understand. God—who was this mysterious

God? *I'd* never seen Him part the sea. *I'd* never heard his voice thunder. All I knew was this list of rules handed to me by another man. He was my parents' God. I didn't know who He was.

Finally, the wandering ended. Moses was dead. My parents were dead. Joshua led us now—but we still weren't sure where we were going. To the river. To the Promised Land. And then what? We fought some battles, all the time knowing they were just warm-ups for the real thing. Across the river sat the big one, basking in its smug walls. How would we ever take Jericho?

Once we actually saw it, any confidence we had sunk past the toes of our sandals. Our spies had been right. The walls did seem to reach to the sky. There was no break in them anywhere. The whole place looked untouchable. And what did we have to fight with? Battering rams and catapults weren't exactly desert wandering equipment. Not too portable. Who were we, with our little army of spears and swords and stones? But if we couldn't beat Jericho, we might as well go back to the desert. It was the only way to Canaan—this land we'd been muddling around for 40 years to reach! What could we do but wait for Joshua to come back from his conference with God?

But when he did come back—what he had to say when he came back. There we all stood, waiting for the great strategic battle plan from our 4-star general. He had to have it! And then, his voice ringing with authority and his face shining like he'd just bathed in pure gold, he gave us the plan. We would walk around the city once a day for six days; then on the seventh day we'd circle it seven times. We'd make a lot of noise that seventh time, with horns and shouting and singing, and the city wall would fall down flat, all by itself. End of plan.

I remember muttering something about Joshua being out in the sun too long. This was no plan at all. It was a suicide mission! As soon as the enemy noticed us snaking around the city in one big line of Israelites, it would be party time for them. They could attack and slaughter us! They wouldn't even have to leave the city. Would I be a part of this craziness? But everyone else was going to do it. Might as well die in glory, I thought. Better there than the desert. Maybe we could be slaves in Canaan instead of Egypt. So we marched.

Then we marched the final day, six times. Each time we marched a little faster, impatient for the last. The seventh time though, we suddenly slowed. Was it a march of majesty, or were we just afraid to get to the end? What was behind all of those suddenly serious faces?

Finally, Joshua gave the sign. The horns trumpeted, the people shouted. I yelled too—what did I have to lose? And then, beneath my feet, the ground began to tremble. I looked up and saw the pebbles trickling down the wall. The rocks started sliding, one by one, then too fast to count, falling one on top of the other, until the air was filled with dust and the noise of shouting, screaming, crashing. The wall—the wall that had reached to the sky—in one moment, fell down flat, touched by no human hand. And in the midst of the dust and cries, I saw something more than a toppled wall. I saw God. God! The God my parents saw. The God Moses saw. The God who saw me—and didn't strike me down dead for my unbelief. This God was no rule book. He was no question on a test to get right or wrong. He is the living God! Now I see! Now I understand.

Now I know why my questions sounded so impossible to my parents' ears. Why follow this God? How could they possibly not?

And now, when my children come around and ask, "Why, Daddy, why? Why do you keep trusting when it doesn't look like anyone is in charge of this mess?" I tell them. God handled the sea. God handled the desert. God handled Jericho, my children. He can handle the messes of our lives too.

LONELY AT THE TOP

Theme: Pride in God's kingdom; learning to be content with the pace and the gifts He gives us.

Passage: Numbers 12

Character: Miriam

Related Scripture: 1 Corinthians 12; Philippians 2:1-11; Psalm 131

Suggestions for Use: Miriam could come in up the aisle, shouting her first words—unclean—repeated as often as necessary to reach the front. Then she should speak from somewhere off to the side or below the pulpit area. This is partly because she is still an outcast but mainly because now she deliberately chooses not to be in that place of authority.

"Unclean, unclean, unclean!" I hate that word! For seven days, it's been the only word I could say to another person. Seven days. The longest seven days I've ever endured. A whole week with no one to listen to but myself. I never knew what awful company I could be. But then, perhaps if I had listened to myself more before . . .

I knew . . . I knew it was wrong to speak of my brother that way. But what could it harm? I didn't think he could be hurt. Moses—the great leader of Israel. How could a little grumbling really harm him? I only wanted a small piece of what he had. I would have been clever enough to stop it before it went too far. I didn't think it would cause such an uproar.

Aaron wasn't too difficult to persuade. If we just discredited our brother a little—not enough to cause real damage. Then maybe I . . . we . . . could have a share of what he had. His authority, his respect. His place as number one.

It wasn't fair, after all. Wasn't Moses human? Didn't I, Miriam, diaper his soft little bottom once? Didn't I save his life when the princess brought him up out of the river? Didn't I teach him about God? Then why was I left behind when God handed out the glory? Why was leading the women the best that I could do? Why was no one writing down *my* prophecies? God spoke to me too. But Moses got all the honors.

So I wanted to bring him down some—just down to where I was. His new marriage made it look so simple. He married a Cushite—a black woman, a woman outside the people of Israel. She's a good woman. I had no reason to speak against her. But what has reason got to do with pride? "She's not of our people," I began to whisper in ears. "How could our *leader* marry outside of the chosen?" Whispers travel quickly in the desert.

I discovered then that Moses could be hurt. And that I had done the hurting. He never rebuked me! Never showed anger! How I wished he had! How could his own sister sink so far—for power?! For such a senseless, meaningless, temporary thing! Didn't I have enough? Prophetess? Sister? Leader? What did I want?

So God caused this disease to fall upon me. Caused my skin to change from desert brown to this inhuman, scaly, white mess. Caused the people who loved me to turn away in fear and disgust. Caused this week-long desert in my heart.

It's hard to be proud when you have to cry words of shame. It's hard to lord it over others when you're cast out alone. It's hard to think you know better than God when He's shown you your own soul.

God gave me a place to be. He gave me a job to do. He even blessed me with His words and visions. Once, not so long ago, I was a slave. One who made no decisions, did not dare to dream of ambitions. I had no hope for ever climbing out of a life of dull slavery to whatever or whoever owned me. But I forgot, so soon, that God saved me at all from such a life—that He gave me a dream and a place. It should have been enough for me.

It should have been. But I forgot. Today, they will come for me. Today, I can go back. The seven days are over. My skin soon will be clean. But what about my heart?

THE MORNING AFTER

Theme: God's ability to make us new, and our honesty about needing it.

Passage: Hosea 1:2-3; 3:1-5

Character: Gomer

Related Scripture: Deuteronomy 4:29-31; Luke 15; Psalm 51; Isaiah 55:1-7; 2 Corinthians 5:17; James 4:8-10; Hosea

Suggestions for Use: Gomer is not a street prostitute but more of a high class call-girl. She can afford to pursue only the relationships that will "benefit" her. In the long run, of course, they do not. Do not play her in stereotypical street walker costume (even if you could in your church!), but give her class. Expensive-looking jewelry and dress can be effective, especially if she touches and looks at them in her last two paragraphs as if to say, "This is it?" She stands in a motel room, trying to convince herself she likes her life. She alternates between leaning toward her husband and rejecting him and his message. This contrast of tone should appear clearly as she changes mood. You will need a mirror for the end.

(Putting on discarded wedding ring and looking at it) I told him not to marry me. Told him what I was. What I'd always be. "I'm a whore, Hosea!" Not much delicate small talk there, huh? He just said, "God commands it." What a romantic proposal. "Yeah, Gomer, I'm sure I'll hate it too, but duty calls . . ." He might as well have said that. But what woman with my reputation would argue with a little security? So I married him. Hosea the prophet of God and Gomer the prostitute. Match made in heaven, right?

I tried to do the respectable thing for a while. But you know, when a girl's used to getting her enjoyment where she can, the same-old, same-old gets dull quick. And there were so many other things I still wanted . . .

Why did I have to be God's little object lesson anyway? Why didn't Hosea marry me and then leave me alone? I might've stayed with him and made a go of it if he hadn't had to change me. Kept telling me how God's people were like prostitutes who wouldn't stop running away from Him and doing wrong. So what was that supposed to say about me? I got the message. Hosea was out to change the world—and he wanted to start with me.

It's not that he wasn't good to me. He was, really. Very good, and kind, and

. . . He tried to make me feel, well, different. Special. I mean, to be honest, I think he really wanted us to love each other. You know, he's the only man who never called me a whore. Even when I told him I was one! He'd just say, "I choose to think of you as you can be."

Well I can't be! I'm not special! I know what I am, but at least I'm not lying about it! I can't change. I don't want to change! So I've run away, over and over. And I'll do it again, if he comes back for me. Let him find me one more time with someone else. Why does he keep coming for me, anyway? He could have gotten a divorce by now. Anyone else would have.

What kind of man would keep trying? Why does he keep forgiving? What can he possibly gain from buying back this well-used piece of goods? He talks about God so much. Who is this God of my husband's? Is He anything like this man? Could there be a God like that?

I only know my father's god. The god he taught us all to believe in was called "get what you can while you can." He'd serve whatever god he thought would get him what he wanted. It didn't matter which one it was on what day. Whatever worked best. I guess I come by prostitution naturally, at least. Isn't that what my father always did? So I find whatever man can best serve me. What's the difference between him and me? Is bed-hopping worse than god-hopping?

Hosea should go looking for another god. The one he's got doesn't seem to work too great for him. But he sticks with his God. Just like he sticks with me. Why does he keep coming? Why doesn't he leave me alone?!

(She looks at herself, her clothes, the room. Turns to a mirror, obviously emotional now.) Alone? Does he know how I feel on a morning like this? When I've gotten my money, my perfume, whatever it was I went hunting for—and I'm alone? The times I'd die to see him coming after me again—but I'd never show it? Gomer, you say you're honest, but you're not. If you were, you'd admit there are more days like this than the others. More times when you know it wasn't worth selling your soul.

He acts like he knows better than I do what I need. God, what do I need? Is this all there is to me? Will I really never be anything but Gomer the town whore? "I choose to think of you as you can be." I don't *know* what I can be. Hosea, would your God forgive like you do? Are you coming? Hosea . . . are you coming for me again?

ONE-MAN WOMAN

Theme: God's ability to put together our pieces, forgiving and restoring.

Passage: John 4

Character: Woman at the well

Related Scripture: Psalms 103; 148:8-18; Ephesians 2:1-10; Hebrews 4:14-16

(Sings) "Praise the name of Jesus. Praise the name of Jesus. He's my . . ." What? Yes, that's right. I did say "Jesus." Loud and clear. I say it all the time. I'm not much of a singer, but I sing it a lot too. Dead? Oh no—I mean, yes, I know what happened. But no, He's not dead. *(Laughs)* Sure, you can call me a silly superstitious woman if you want to. I've been called worse. I know most people don't believe. But if you knew what He did for me, you might understand. Maybe you'd know why I'm not surprised He could rise from the dead.

It didn't happen that long ago. But it seems like another life. That other woman who lived that life—she isn't me anymore. I remember feeling tired that afternoon. I felt tired a lot. "Change of life," my friends said. But that wasn't it. What I needed was a change of life. But my life never changed. My boyfriend—he hadn't been too nice that morning. He never was too nice after a night at the bars. Which meant he wasn't very nice most mornings. But then he always said he was sorry. He'd come back every time and say he loved me. So I stayed. I always stayed if they said they loved me. God knows how I tried to believe it.

They didn't all beat me, like John. They didn't even all drink. They were just men willing to hook up with a woman no one else wanted. Five husbands in 18 years. Must be a record, you think? You s'pose they'd put me in the *Jerusalem Inquirer?* No, guess not. Not even they'd take a half-breed like me.

I only knew Benny three weeks before I married him. I shouldn't have been so surprised when he drifted out just like he drifted in. I kept thinking . . . This time, this time, this one'll stay. This one will love me. I can belong to this one for good. They all said I was special. They all told me I was beautiful, desirable. They told me they loved me, that I was the only one for them. Then why didn't they stay? If I was so wonderful, why did Joe have to go to the red-light district? Why did Ed have to live at the bar? What was wrong with me? Why couldn't anyone love me?

For years, I tried to have a baby with one of them. I thought, at least one person will love me. A baby—a baby has to love me. Has to belong to me. Maybe if it was a boy—maybe his daddy would even love me. Anyway, I wouldn't be alone. But it never happened. I couldn't even do what all women are s'posed to be able to do. What good was I anyway? Who really cared who beat me up or cheated on me?

Like I said, John roughed me up that morning, so I didn't go out to get water with the other women. They never talked to me anyway, so I liked to wait. And when I got there, there was this Man. Another passer-through? But He was a Jew. What was He doing coming to our well, the home of the half-breeds Jews despised so much? I couldn't help looking, hoping He wouldn't notice. Not that He would ever have said two words to me. Only a certain kind of man ever spoke to me, and I could tell He wasn't that kind. What was a Jewish man doing at the watering hole of Samaritan women? Strange, strange man.

Then He did something even more amazing. He spoke to me! Asked for water from me. From me—a woman he might have just cursed or spit at if he knew what I was. But when He looked at me . . . I felt like He did know who I was. Then why didn't He turn away?

We talked a bit, about things I thought would interest a Jew. I tried to keep cool, but my nerves were dancin' the two-step. The conversation kept turning toward me. Why would anyone want to talk about me, anyway? But I kept feeling like He did. I sure didn't! I wasn't exposing my worthless life to this Man. I felt like I would die right there if that Man had to know all I'd done and been. I can't explain it. I just knew the shame would kill me.

Then He told me. "You've had five husbands, and the one you have now is not your husband." I wanted to deny it. "No!" I wanted to cry. "You don't understand. I just wanted to be loved! I just wanted to be something to someone. Don't! Don't . . ." But, right when I nearly turned and ran, I looked again. And just when I wanted to hide from His eyes, I saw His eyes hurt too. He did understand. He knew all about me. And still He did understand. And He . . . He loved me. He loved me without saying a word. Without making all those promises other men had made. He didn't ask for a thing. And suddenly I wanted to give Him everything—to pour out all my worthlessness and beg him to put the pieces back together.

But I froze. All I could say was, "Sir, I perceive You are a prophet." A prophet! More than a prophet! Before He told me, I knew. This Man was the Messiah! The One all our people had waited for! The One who would make all things right. But not just that. He was the One I had been waiting for. He would make all things right for me. He could change my life. I could belong to Him. And I knew I would never have to search again for who I was. I could be His.

How do I know He's alive again? Because He gave me my life. It's not hard to believe. If He could resurrect this soul-dead woman, He could beat something as small as death. He is alive. And I am too. What more do you need to know?

(Sings) "Praise the name of Jesus. He's my rock. He's my fortress. He's my deliverer; in Him will I trust. Praise the name of . . ."

LOVE, HONOR, . . . AND OBEY?

Theme: Honoring parents (or government, employers, etc.) when their commands conflict with conscience. What's the right choice when two options could be right?

Passage: 1 Samuel 18:1-9; 19:1-10

Character: Jonathan

Related Scripture: John 16:12-15; James 1:5

Honor your father and mother. Honor your father and mother. Honor . . . I know, I know! I've heard it since before I knew what "honor" meant! I've memorized it! *(Recites mechanically)* The fifth commandment. "Thou shalt honor thy father and mother that thy days may be prolonged." OK? So stop hammering at me with it. I'll write it 100 times. Just leave me alone!

Haven't I always done my best on that one? I picked up my toys when Mom said, "Jonathan, time for bed." I never complained when I was 13 and Dad insisted on giving me a big bear hug in front of all my friends. Talk about embarrassed! And sore too. Man, Dad can still hug. I let him pick out my wife, my home, my future. Now he wants to pick my best friend. How much can I honor, anyway?

David and me, we've always been best buds, ever since Dad brought him home. "Friends for life," we used to swear a secret boys' oath. Yeah, it seemed unlikely to other people I guess. The king's son and the little shepherd scrub-work boy.

If Dad had known what that boy would be. GQ looks combined with a warrior's heart for God. He couldn't help but catch the peoples' attention—and then their hearts. Dad gloried in it too, since David was "his boy"—until he realized what it all meant. His grip on adoration was slipping—while David's soared. A new king? It doesn't look so unlikely anymore. Especially since God seems to be convinced David is the man for the job. My friend the king. Of course, I should have been the next king. But I don't really mind. I've seen first-hand what that job is like.

But Dad hasn't been so accepting. He is king, after all, and he wants to stay that way. So he's trying to murder my best friend. God, what do I do? Why stick me in the middle of this triangle of insanity? What did I ever do but try to love them both?

God, I said I knew what honor meant. I don't! I thought it meant just go along, do as he says, don't cause any waves. But how can I go along with this? My father wants to kill my best friend! And I'm supposed to rubber stamp that "OK"? How far does this honoring stuff go? Isn't honor just for parents who do the right things? How can God have meant it for all parents, all the time? Didn't He know some wouldn't deserve it? C'mon God, look at the facts. Some parents just aren't honor material. What then? It's hard to honor a dad who wants to nail your best friend to the wall. Literally.

But . . . it's hard not to honor him too. I love him, God. He's been a good father, really. I can't forget all that for the past few months of insanity. How can I turn my back on him when he needs me? He needs someone to be on his side now. That should be me—his oldest son. Part of the reason he wants to kill David is to keep the throne for me. He wants me to inherit all this. What kind of gratitude am I thinking of? What will it do to him if I turn away too? Is that honoring? To put a friend over the man who's given me everything? God, I can't turn on either one of them! Yes—Dad's wrong this time! I know he's wrong! I just don't know what's right for *me* to do.

It sounded so easy in the commandments. But what do I do when it's not so easy? What do I obey? The command or the conscience? I can't do both. Can I? Can I honor my father and save my friend too? Is there a right answer on this test? What is the choice when two rights collide in one colossal wrong?

WHO WAS THAT MAN?

Theme: The sadness of encountering God and never really knowing who it was.

Passage: Luke 17:11-19

Character: One of the 10 lepers

Related Scripture: 1 John 5:20-21; 1 Chronicles 28:9; Psalm 100; Hosea 6:3; John 17:1-18

Suggestions for Use: You will need a table and chair.

(Walking across stage area) Hey, Ruth! Hannah! Sammy! I'm home! Yeah—it's me—Reuben! Ruth—can you believe it? No, don't be afraid. I'm not sick anymore. See? Ain't it great? I'm free! Free at last, thank God almighty, I'm free at last . . . Huh? God? Well, I didn't . . . It's just a song you know. I don't know if He . . . Well I guess, I guess He must have done it. Haven't thought much about that. But I'll be sure to put it in my prayers tonight, OK? Thank You, God!

Course, my prayers are kinda rusty. Out there livin' away from everybody else we didn't pray too much. It gets lonely, Ruth. Really lonely. Prayers don't seem to make much difference out there. I quit a long time ago. What? You didn't? Well, maybe. Maybe it was God.

Really though, it was this guy. We, a bunch of us, heard He could do miracle stuff. You know, like magic tricks. He was healin' people all over the place. Gettin' thick as matzo balls, they wuz. So we thought, what's to lose? We went and asked Him to make us not lepers anymore. What He said kinda let us down a little. He didn't wave His hands or say any magic words and make us all OK. He said, "Go show yourselves to the priests so they can pronounce you clean."

But we weren't clean. Any dummy, let alone a priest, could see that. What was goin' on? He sounded like He really knew what He was talkin' about though, and He had this great reputation and all. Besides, like I said, what's to lose? So we did like He said. And hey, Ruth, guess what? It disappeared—while we were walkin'! First Bob, he says, "Hey—no white spots!" Then Abe goes, "Whoa—me too!" And all 10 of us look at our hands and each others' faces. I tell you, we had a party right there on that hill! We just jumped and hugged and yelled—the best party I've ever been to. We could go back home! See our families. Be real people again! Then we all started bawlin' like babies. We wuz so happy.

It's good to be home, Ruth. I missed you. Eat? Eat a meal not cooked by a bunch of leper guys? Pass a plate! *(Walks to table and sits) That* looks like food! You know, Ruth, somethin' about this whole thing is buggin' me though. I just can't figure out what it is. It's like I forgot something. I don't know.

I wonder who that guy was, anyway. Jesus Son of something . . . I can't remember. Didn't quite catch it. Maybe it was even Jonah, or Jesse, or . . . I don't know. Maybe I should've gone back and said thanks like Aaron did. Always did have good manners, that Aaron. But I just wanted to get home.

I really wonder who He was. Maybe it would've been important to know. Oh well, what difference does it make now? Pass me that pumpkin pie, will ya, Ruth?

CATCH ME LATER

Theme: Being too busy for what's important, especially for bringing children to Jesus.

Passage: Matthew 21:1-11

Character: A child witnessing Palm Sunday

Related Scripture: Psalm 148; Luke 10:38-41; 18:15-17

Suggestions for Use: The character is a child, but it may be difficult to find a child capable of dramatic monologue. A young adult can play the part, provided he or she uses the excited, urgent, passionate tone and manner of a child.

(Runs in to one side of stage) Mom, Mom, guess what? It was so neat! Mom, come see! You've got to come see this! But . . . but . . . I can't tell you. It's . . . you've just got to *see* it. Please come, Mom. Can't you do the dishes later? OK, I'll try to tell you, but . . .

There were all these people. No, I didn't get in the way. So many people I couldn't see anything! Of course I didn't push. Well, maybe. Just a little. But everyone else was too. But Mom—they didn't care. They were all singing and laughing. No, I didn't talk to strangers. Well, Mom, everybody was talking!

Someone was coming down the road. No, I don't know who it was. I couldn't see! But He must've been important. A bunch of other kids ran to cut some branches, so I went, too, so I could do it. No, I didn't play with a knife. Mo-o-o-om! Just come see! He'll be gone soon if you don't come! I don't know who! Can you come tell me? I want to know! No, I didn't get all dirty cutting leaves. I don't want to wash my hands for lunch! I want to go back!

Please, Mom. It was like a big birthday party! No, you wouldn't have to change clothes. Lots of people singing and waving those branches in the air! *(Singsong)* "Hosanna, hosanna to the King." Yes, they did say, "King." No, I'm not making it up. It is too what they said! No, Mom, I didn't mean to talk back. You don't want to come? You'd have fun, Mom. You really should meet Him. He must be someone pretty special. Can I go see Daddy, then? Yes, I'll tell him lunch is ready. Bye, Mom!

Dad, Dad! No, it's not time for lunch. I mean—maybe—but, but . . . Dad, did you hear all that noise? There's a big parade! Can you come quick, Dad?

Maybe you could put me on your shoulders so I could see. I couldn't see anything. But it's so much fun. Oh Dad, you can do your order later. You always get them done. Maybe I could come back and help you after it's all over. Yeah, I remember last time. But I won't goof up again, I promise. Can't you come, quick? You can come back to work. Everyone's going!

I don't know why. It's this Man. He's coming up the road, and they're all singing and laughing and throwing things at Him. No, I mean nice things. They like Him, Dad. I don't know who He is. Hurry, Dad, take me down there. You can find out! I want to know! They called Him, I think, something like Son of David. I don't know. Do you think they meant your Uncle David? Well, I didn't mean to be silly. I didn't know. Dad, just come. I'll show you. Why? Why do I have to stay away? They're not dangerous—they're singing! Won't you come, please? I really want you . . . OK, see you at dinner. Bye, Dad.

Hey, Zach, where you goin'? Yeah—I been there already. It is neat. It's . . . it's . . . a big parade and a party and, and . . . Sure I'll go back with you. Maybe we could climb a tree or something. I don't know who He is. Maybe someone there will tell us. I sure wish my mom and dad would come. They're busy. But someone will tell us. There's got to be somebody there who knows who He is.

THE THINGS TIME CHANGES

Theme: Unity. What has happened to the racial, social, and economic unity that characterized the Early Church?

Passage: Mark 15:21; Romans 16:13* (See explanation below)

Character: Wife of Simon of Cyrene

Related Scripture: John 17:20-23; Acts 10:34-35; Ephesians 2:11-22; Revelation 7:9-12; Psalm 133; Proverbs 22:2

Suggestions for Use: An older woman sits at a table and writes this letter. She reads as she writes. Act as if you are writing, moving the pen, taking up pages and looking at them, even crossing out words. Do not, however, read slowly as if the words were just coming. The woman is black, but do not let that stand in the way of using whoever is available to play her.

*Rufus appears two places in the Bible. He is mentioned as the son of Simon of Cyrene, the man who carried Jesus' cross. Later, Paul greets a man named Rufus in the Roman church. Are they the same person? Not necessarily, of course. But some scholars are persuaded that they are. Paul mentions Rufus's mother as someone "who has been a mother to me, too." Therefore, she must have known Paul somewhere else previously before traveling to Rome to be greeted in his letter.

Dear Rufus,

Well, Son, how's life in Rome treating you? Quite a change from home, isn't it? But I guess you're used to moving around. With your father's job, we never put down roots for too long, did we? I'm just glad he landed us here before he went. I do still miss him so. I guess it takes a long time. Thanks again for the offer to come live with you. I may just do that sometime. We'll see about it.

But what a family Simon left me to stay with here! I had Lydia over for coffee the other morning. We always talk so long—seems it takes all day to have coffee when she comes! Let's see . . . I just finished making that outfit for Ruth's new baby. So many children they have and so little money. But they've such a kind spirit. I like to help however I can. Then we had a visiting preacher two weeks ago. It's always good to hear from someone new. Joey is getting married. (Guess I'll have to stop calling him Joey then; he's quite grown up.) I suppose you're not making any plans like that yet?

Did I tell you Paul came through last month? On another of his whirlwind trips again. Can't help wishing you wouldn't go on some of those kinds of trips, but I know you have to listen to the Lord.

It's just that you know our friend Paul—he never takes care of himself. Every time he comes around I got to take him in for as long as he'll let me and fatten him up. He works so hard! I keep tellin' him, "Paul, you'd cover more miles if you'd just take some time for yourself. Get some decent food and rest. Get yourself a wife! You know what your mother would say." He always laughs. "You're the best mother I have," he smiles at me. "Besides, I cover the miles enough with God's help, don't you think?" And how can I argue? He always does.

Imagine, Rufus, me, this old, black, foreign lady being called "Mom" by the likes of Paul. Before I met these Christians, a man like him would cross the street to make sure he didn't touch me. But here? That's what I mean about this place. In all the places we've been, I've never seen anywhere like it. The other day I brought supper to Thaddeus. Since when would I have been let in a white Roman door, except maybe as a slave? What is this new world Jesus let us into?

Oh Son, I'm so glad for the day you "accidentally" ran into that Roman death march. Could you have known that bleeding, helpless Man would help us all more than we ever knew we needed? I'm not so sad when I think that your father's gone to be with Him. But if he had left me alone anywhere else, with any other people but these Christians, who knows what would have happened to me? They don't take care of old widows out there in that world, black or white. And the money will run out eventually, even though your father did well. But here among my brothers and sisters, we all take care of each other.

Paul said something about that when he was here once. He said, "Mother, there is no slave or free, black or white, man or woman—or anything in Jesus. We're all bought with the same price. Each one of us was worth the same amount of His blood." I said, "That's good Paul, you should write that down." He said he thought he would.

But they really mean that here, Rufus. It's not just talk. Young and old people, rich and poor, black and white—we all sit together and work together and no one says I'm worth less than anyone else. I wonder if it's like that in the other churches? How about Rome? It's hard to imagine a whole world working that way.

Rufus, suppose Jesus doesn't come back real soon? Suppose He waits a while, for more people? Do you think we can keep it up? Having everyone together like this? I don't think anyone's ever tried anything like this before, Son. But who could if Jesus' people can't? Sure we can. I'll bet . . . I'll bet if He waits, oh, 2,000 years—things will be just the same. The Church won't change. It'll just get better. And bigger. People like me—we'll always feel right at home.

Well, I'd best go now, Son. I've got pies in the oven, and it's getting late. Say hello to Phoebe.

Love,
Mom

SUCH A DEAL

Theme: Reaping what we sow

Passage: Genesis 29:14-30

Character: Laban

Related Scripture: Proverbs 5:21-23; 11:3-6; Psalm 15; Galatians 6:7-10

Benny! Such a deal I got for you! Look at this little model! Only two years old and fully equipped. Low mileage. Gorgeous color. Whaddya mean, am I sure she's only two? Is my name Laban, or not? You got my word. Fifty bucks. You take her home, gas her up. Best little sheep you'll ever get for the money. Yeah, it's a deal. Throw in a bale of this sweet grass too. Best grass this side of Chicago. No weeds in there, you got my word.

Hey, Gus, you old ram's horn, you! How's the wife? What goat? Last week? I sold you a goat last week? Oh! That goat! How's she doin'? Dry? Oh no, Gus, that can't be. Why, that little goat was givin' my wife a gallon of milk a day at least! Sure, why just the day before you bought her, my girl Leah, she says, "That goat makes the best cheese, Dad." My word—of course. Whaddya mean, did Leah get the right goat? My daughter is *not* near-sighted!

You sure you're feeding her all right? Maybe you want to buy some of the best grass this side of . . . Just trying to help, my friend. Now, Gus, a deal's a deal. That's business. Maybe she's just gettin' used to a new place. Tell you what—you stop by the house and tell Hannah I said to give you a hunk of that good cheese and some milk. We'll see you later, Gus. Got a customer. Gotta go.

Jacob, my boy. How's business? Busy? No, I'm never too busy for you, my friend. You're family! Taking good care of my merchandise out there? I promised a good black sheep to Lou over the hill. Pick one out for me, will you? You know what to look for. Yeah, don't need to tell you. What about that one that keeps losing her lambs? We'll never get any stock out of her. Bring her on up here.

You want to talk? Serious? Why Jake, my friend, what could be so serious on a day like today? The sun is shining, the grass is green, I just unloaded, sold, that old white sheep. What could be so serious? Marriage? That is serious. My daughter? Well, maybe we could work something out. You're a healthy young man. Good stock for the family. Have I got a deal for you. She can cook. She can clean. She can manage money. Never wastes a penny, that's my Leah. The best deal in a wife you'll find this side of . . . What? Not Leah? Rachel? You want Rachel? Well, I don't know. Sure, she's a pretty face, Jake, but how does she run? I tell you, if you want a deal take Leah.

I'm only trying to be your friend. Would I steer you wrong? Take it from me, I've been in this marriage business longer than you. I know what you need. Love? Oh, you're in love. Of course. Young love, it's so . . . how're you gonna feel in 10 years though? You gotta think about these things, Jake. OK, OK, you want Rachel. We'll talk. We'll work something out. You leave it to me.

Whaddya mean, you want it in writing? A guarantee? From me, your Uncle Laban? Haven't I always done good by you? You got my word. What else do you want? Well, yeah, but Jacob, that's business. You know how business is. Let the buyer beware. You gotta get by. Why—do you know what would happen to me if I got honest about every little thing I sell off this lot? It's the way things are—they all know it too. They know how the world works.

But you're family! I would never treat my favorite nephew like that! Well, yeah, there was that time my cousin Josh came by. Sure, I sheared those sheep a bit before I sold them to him. But he had it coming, you know. Besides, it'll all grow back. I wouldn't do that to you. You got my word.

Now, Jake, if you're going to get picky about this honesty stuff. You know, you don't have the best record yourself. I mean, Josh's my cousin. But you—you cheated your brother! Out of a lot more than a lousy little bit of wool! Never mind how I know. I find these things out. Come to think about it, my sister, your mother, she's quite the schemer herself. Must run in the family. You've been playing the game with me here a long time. You understand the rules. You work 'em better than most guys I know. So what's the sudden push for honesty?

Yeah, marriage is different. That's what I said before. I wouldn't cheat you about something like that. You can trust me. OK, OK, I'll put it in writing. We'll get something done up. It's a deal. Now go on, get back out there and get me that little black sheep.

(*Shakes hand and mutters, then turns to greet another person*) Gus—back so soon. How'd it go up at the house? You talked to Rachel? But I said . . . wasn't Hannah around? Rachel give you the cheese? She gave you what? Your money back?! How'd you . . . you told her I *said* to give you your money back? No way. Rachel knows I would never . . . You told her Jacob said to do it? And she did. Of course. But you didn't really talk to Ja—. . . Gus, that was low. You lied to my daughter. Yeah, yeah, I know. Business is business. Live by the sword, die by the sword. You got me fair and square, Gus. No hard feelings.

(*Turns and begins talking to self*) Live by the sword . . . Yeah, that's the way it is all right. You're going to take; you're going to get taken. Good thing it doesn't happen to me very often. I'm too good at this.

(*Walks across stage, as if to house*) Hey, Leah! My oldest, my favorite child. Haven't you always wanted to get married? Well, have I got a deal for you . . .

WHEN I GROW UP

Theme: Sanctity of life. What is the potential of the world's throwaway children?

Passage: Exodus 2:1-10

Character: Pharaoh's daughter

Related Scripture: Psalm 139:13-16; Genesis 9:6; Matthew 10:29-31

Suggestions for Use: You will need a basket with a small blanket inside.

What is that, over there? I think it's—it's a basket. And a carefully made one, too, I'd say. Why would anyone put such a beautiful basket in the river? But what . . . ? There's something in there—I can hear it. *(She goes over and kneels down beside the basket, pulling back the cover.)* It's . . . it's . . . *(Her shock turns to a smile as she looks on a baby's face.)* Oh, the poor little one—out here all alone! He must be so frightened. I'd cry, too, sweet baby, if I were lost alone in this big world. But someone took care of you. Even in this river, you're not one bit wet.

(Turns to address person beside her) What? Shall I call whom? My father's soldiers? Whatever for? Yes, I know he looks like a Hebrew child; that's plain enough, but . . . OH. A Hebrew child. A Hebrew *boy* child. I had forgotten my father's orders.

Look at those perfect little fingers! They look so strong. What great things might he use those hands for? He's reaching for me, don't you see? I suppose he really wants to play with my earrings. Do you like their glittering, little one? How could anyone want to still those tiny hands?

My father's orders. Kill the Hebrew boy babies. All of them. I suppose I knew it was being done. It is a serious problem, after all. Those people are overrunning the country, they're having so many babies. And they can barely feed the ones they have.

Still, this one . . . Look at that little mouth. He smiled at me! What words might come from that mouth someday? Who might be charmed by that smile? How can such a little baby be a problem?

Father says they're an economic burden. He says they're only slum kids anyway, never amount to anything more. We'll all be better off if we keep only the ones we can take care of.

Better off? To shut those trusting eyes, the color of rich, dark honey? You've stopped crying, haven't you? Did you only want someone to care for you? Those eyes—looking at me for help. Might those eyes flash one day and move more hearts than mine? Father's orders made sense until I saw this child. Now . . . now I can see nothing but him.

(Stands) No, we will not call my father's soldiers. The baby is mine. He will stay mine. This child will not die. Look—he smiled again. He knows. He knows he can trust me.

(Kneels close again) I will call him Moses, because I drew him out of the water. What do you think, what will my Moses be? How will he use those hands and mouth and eyes? Will he build palaces or play music? Will he shout great speeches or sing sweet songs? Will he move men to obey with a look, or women to follow? What do you think, my Moses? Your life is worth more than slavery or death. What might you be, my little baby?

WHO CARES ABOUT AUNT LEAH?

Theme: Slowing the holiday rush to remember why we celebrate.

Passage: Leviticus 23:33-43

Character: Old Testament wife during Feast of Tabernacles

Related Scripture: Luke 10:38-41; Matthew 11:28-30; Psalms 95:1-7; 98; 100; 150

Suggestions for Use: Thanksgiving is clearly suggested, though the entire season before Christmas could work. She needs a couple of boxes strewn around and a Bible.

Where is the soup kettle? Who packed the yams? What do you mean, they're in with the dog's food? I suppose next you'll be telling me you packed the dirty socks too. Is the meat going to keep? This weather certainly isn't helping. Did you put it in the cooler? What do you mean there's no room? Well what is you father's film doing in there? I don't care if it works better cold. Put in the turkey!

Why do we do this every year anyway? It's work enough to get a dinner together in my own kitchen. But to pack up housekeeping and go live in a tent for a week? What's the point? What a ridiculous custom. We only do it because your father's father's father did it. I'll bet Great-Grandma wasn't too crazy about the idea either.

Cut the branches. Buy the turkey. Gather the fruit. Shop for chestnuts— cheap! Unpack the dishes. Find out what kind of pie Uncle Myron can eat with his blood pressure. Build a tent. A big tent! Go shopping. Go harvesting. Go, go, go! And after it's all over, who does the dishes?

And then there's living in a tent for a week with your Uncle Eli and Aunt Leah. I know he's going to smoke those cigars right inside where we all have to breathe it. And she's going to spend all week telling me how the baby knows long division and read *War and Peace* last week, while my teenagers are still having trouble with "wash in cold water, line dry."

Why do we do this? Someday, someday women are going to rebel. We're not always going to stand for this. Someday we're going to have rights—and then! Then no one is going to make us spend weeks getting ready for holidays and days getting over them!

Why am I doing this? Oh yes, God commanded it. But what on earth for? To punish women for Eden? What? Pack the Bible? Why? Well, I didn't really mean . . . I'm sure God had His reasons, but I'm a little too busy to read up on it just now. Ask your father. It's probably in there in one of those long, boring books. Leviteronomy or Deutikiah or something like that.

Well, go ahead and pack it if you want to. Just don't put it in the cooler. What could God possibly have been thinking of? Go find your sister's shoes, will you? A *pair* please. Not like last time. She wandered around all week with one green tennis shoe and one Mary Jane. I'm sure Aunt Leah had a good laugh over that one. Here's what? The what? The Feast of Tabernacles? Yes, that's what we're supposed to be managing all right. The Week of Chaos, more like. It's actually in there, huh? Go get the shoes now. Hurry. *(Keeps packing, but getting slower and slower, glancing at Bible several times)*

What does that thing have to say, anyway? *(Picks up Bible and sits on box.)*

"So beginning with the fifteenth day of the seventh month, after you have gathered the crops of the land, celebrate the festival to the LORD for seven days; the first day is a day of rest, and the eighth day is also a day of rest . . . take choice fruit from the trees, and palm fronds, [and] leafy branches and rejoice before the LORD your God for seven days. . . . This is to be a lasting ordinance for the generations to come; celebrate it . . ."

Resting? Celebrating? *(Looks mystified)* Celebration? Rest? *(Stands and walks among boxes, thinking and shaking head. Turns finally.)* You found the shoes? Good. You know what? You think you could find my old tambourine? I know—it's packed away somewhere. Haven't used it in . . . I don't know. And your father's guitar? Sure—let's bring those firecrackers left over from the summer! What do you think—what would happen if we took paper plates instead of all these dishes to wash? Who cares what Aunt Leah would say? C'mon let's finish packing. Your dad will be home soon. Let's be ready to go.

A SIMPLE QUESTION

Theme: Christ's call to abandon our security and follow Him.

Passage: Mark 10:17-27

Character: Rich young man

Related Scripture: Matthew 6:19-33; 16:24-26; Deuteronomy 15:7-11; Isaiah 58:6-11; Psalm 112

Suggestions for Use: Man sits at table on which money is piled, the larger the piles, the better. He is counting and sorting them. He will need a table, chair, and play money.

(Singsong) "The king was in his counting house . . ." Let's see, 10 percent to the church. Right off the top. Gross income. Just like God says. Ten for Maggie. Oh, make it 12. She's been a good wife this week. Then there're the bills, and the kids' lessons, and 10 to save. . . . That leaves . . . 25 for me! *(Shoves almost all the money into "his" pile, leaving others with a little left over)* Good thing, too, because I already ordered that CD I had my eye on. Looks like just about enough set aside for that new red Jeep Cherokee too. Course Maggie wants an Arrowstar, but . . . hey, things are going so well—we'll be able to do both before you know it! Yes, sir, God's really blessing me.

(Hums song again) He is, you know. No matter what that Teacher said. Wish I could get Him out of my mind. What did He want from me, anyway? I only asked a simple question. I really meant it too. I want to do what makes God happy. Don't I give my tithe? I go to church. I've never cheated on my wife. I've looked a little, but I absolutely have not cheated. Everyone around would say what a great guy I am. What did He want?

I just asked one thing. What do I have to do to go to heaven? A simple question. Just give me a simple answer. But He doesn't. "Go, sell all you have, and give to the poor," He says. What? Did he want my kids to go barefoot? My wife to ride a bicycle? What would poor people do with all my money, anyway? They'd only waste it on junk and then be poor again. I know how to handle my money. That's why God gave it to me. After all, my money's pretty useful to the church. I bought that new keyboard for youth meetings. It's not like I don't give to God.

What more did He want me to do? *(Stands and paces)* I've kept all of God's commands. I check them every day to make sure. Well, almost every day. But this giving everything away business . . . that's not in here! God never said anything about that! How did He come up with such a thing?

Maybe if I increase my tithe. Maybe 12 percent. Or even 15. Maybe that's what He meant. Or, I could set aside a little bit for charity. Sure—I'll go down to the mall and get a name of one of those poor kids. That should make Him happy. I can wait for that CD for a week. There's a lot of stuff I can do that shouldn't take too much . . . might even be fun. *(Moves small portion of pile to other side as he speaks. Looks again at a large pile still remaining on his side.)* Might even have to wait a month or two for the Arrowstar. But the Cherokee . . . well, that's on sale this week. Can't let that get by. Good stewardship to buy it now, you know.

(Paces again) I wish I could just forget I ever met Him. I just know He meant something . . . something I don't understand. Couldn't He just give me something to do, some rule to live by? Some percent off the top so I'd know where I stood? "Give it all and follow Me." What does that mean? I can't check that off on a chart. Can't run it through the accounting program on the IBM.

"Give it all and follow Me." Follow where? How? Doesn't sound like solid planning for the future to me. Maybe I should forget Him. It's obvious God is pleased enough with what I've done. Maybe I'm getting too emotional over all this. *(Sits and resumes counting and piling)*

A simple question: What good thing do I have to do to get to heaven? Why couldn't He just give me a simple answer?

THE ONCE—AND FUTURE?—KING

Theme: The need to worship and know Christ as more than a baby at Christmas.

Passage: Matthew 2:1-12

Character: A wise man

Related Scripture: Isaiah 9:2-7; John 1:1-14

Home. How long will it be now until we're home? Not long, I think. This road is beginning to look less foreign, more like a familiar friend. And yet—a part of me feels as if home will be very foreign now. Not ever the same.

It's been a long trip. We packed up some time ago, my friends and I. I can't even remember exactly when. Tracking the days doesn't seem to matter much when each day is the same. Sleeping, walking, eating, sleeping, walking. And talking. Talking about what we were doing, why we came, what on earth we hoped to find.

The star. That glowing, throbbing, silver circle piercing the night sky. I still see it, though it's gone now. Why did it entrance us so, when others hardly noticed it? Oh, they saw it, too, but—why that strange tug that told us it *meant* something? That we must go and see its meaning? Did the gods choose us, for some special reason? Or the God—the One those Hebrews talk about? Why us? But we had to go, and now—now we return.

To what? From what? We found what we came for, I guess. We had heard of the prophecies for a Jewish king. Mighty and powerful—a force for the world to reckon with he would be. But what we found didn't resemble a king much. They were poor, very poor. He wasn't precisely dressed in purple and gold. And the parents—so young, so inexperienced, so . . . so unroyal-like. I've catered to the whims of kings all my life. I know what they're like. And these people weren't like that. A baby. A poor, homely, little baby. That was all.

And yet, they didn't seem surprised when we came. Three of the foreign court's finest, impressive figures in that small, dingy town. More than a few passers-by stared at the procession we made. We descended on these people's doorstep in all our glory, like a figment of their wildest imagination, bringing gifts they'd never dreamed of seeing, let alone owning; and they greet us like we were expected. Nothing special, Mary. Just a few foreign sages with gold bricks to see the baby.

The King of the Jews. The Redeemer of people. Sound asleep, even snoring I believe. Yet we had followed the star, and the prophecies rang true to this place. And His own king certainly didn't believe He was an ordinary child. There He was. The sleeping King. Something pulled inside of me, the way it had when I saw the star. It was true. He was something to worship. But what would He become?

How can I just pack it all up and go back? Back where? Home? They don't know the world has changed! The things we've seen, all we've learned—they mean nothing to anyone there. It's business as usual for them. They won't even know, or care, that nothing will ever be the same.

And what am I to tell them? That the King who will change everything is a baby? With a peasant girl and a carpenter for parents? And if anyone did believe me, what would I tell them to do? Who would I say He really is? I don't know myself! He will grow up. He will do something. Be something. But what? I must know those things too. I can't just continue to worship a baby!

I can see the city lights from here. A baby will be hard to remember in their glare. I wanted to stay. I didn't want to go back into this foreign world with just a baby. It won't be enough. I'm afraid I will forget that I am supposed to have changed. I wanted to learn, to see and hear His life. What kind of king will that baby be?

IN HIS HANDS

Theme: Trusting the Lord with our children

Passage: 1 Samuel 1

Character: Hannah

Related Scripture: Deuteronomy 6:1-9; 11:18-21; Proverbs 22:6; Psalm 139:1-16; Isaiah 49:15-18

Suggestions for Use: Hannah sits as if at a sewing machine or cutting cloth.

The boy is growing so fast. It's hard to know what size he'll be when I see him next. Oh, Samuel, what will you look like this year? Will you have grown two inches? Three? Or four? Will your father's quick black eyes look out of your little-boy face? It seemed last year you were growing to favor him more and more. You'll be taller than him one day, though—but then we're not such big people, your father and I.

Will those eyes be excited to see me? I'm so afraid that someday you won't care if your mother comes. I'm such a small part of your life. You're learning every day the things of God, and me . . . hardly able to leave the cares of home to come see you. Do you know, my faraway child, how much I love you? Do you understand how it tears every bit of my heart to go and leave you there after I've come? I try to keep you from seeing the tears. Maybe I shouldn't. I want so badly to snatch you away, to take you home and be your mother all the time, not just one day a year.

The neighbors, they say, "Oh Hannah, you're so blessed. A son in service to God and more left at home to take his place. No one is so lucky as you." Take your place?! You are my firstborn, my prayed for, anguished for child. How could anyone ever take your place, from the moment you came into my world?

How are they caring for you, Samuel? I know you're being fed, taught, clothed. You're growing strong and important. But are you growing good, my child? I fear for you in that place. I fear for your heart, your spirit. Is it foolish to be afraid you'll grow up bad when you're living right there in God's house?

But I do worry. Eli hasn't done so well by his own sons. They are not good men, Samuel, though I shouldn't say it. How do I know he will do any better with you? Won't he make the same mistakes, do it all the same way? Will he change my sweet child into the selfish, careless men his own children are? Eli is a good man. He is not like his sons. But how do I know he knows how to raise *my* son?

My son. But you are not all my son. I've also known that since you came into this house. I promised you to God. It was only because of Him that I ever had any part of you at all. I should be glad for the one day a year. I would have had nothing without His help.

I promised you to Him, and I let you go. Why can't I let Him keep you? Why can't I let you go all the way? I trust God, but . . . still these worries, the doubts. Did I do the right thing? Am I being the mother I should be? Are you going to turn out all right, in spite of it all?

O Lord, I want to trust You. I want to leave him in Your hands. But, God, do You know how I feel? Do You understand my fear? How I long for him to be with me? Do You know what it's like to give up a son You love? Do You really understand?